THE GI BILL
1946-1951

Audrey Fahlberg

THE GI BILL
1946-1951

University of Wisconsin
Badger Village

Audrey Syse Fahlberg

Rev. date: 01/23/2020

To order additional copies of this book, contact:
Xlibris
1-888-795-4274
www.Xlibris.com
Orders@Xlibris.com
807410

THE GI BILL

I dedicate this book in memory of Willson J. Fahlberg, Sr.
"my Will" for seventy-three years of marriage—also known
as "Poppy" to many in our family of five generations.

1946

Today is a frigid thirty-degree day in January, not the best day for moving. The highway is covered in ice and snow. We leave our cozy apartment on Monroe Street in Madison, a few blocks from the University of Wisconsin, and move thirty-five miles north to a place called Badger Village. The University of Wisconsin acquired the whole village in order to provide housing for veterans returning from World War II and are registered at the university to study under the GI Bill.

In November of 1945, when we visited Badger Village, we rented 71F—an end unit in a long building of four apartments located near the school and the playground. Moving a few blocks from the university to the country seems like a crazy idea to many. To us, it is an opportunity for growth. We pray God has a Master Plan for our family.

We see the sign University of Wisconsin Badger Village and turn off Highway 12 to be greeted by a postcard scene. The old row houses are snow covered; there's smoke from wood-burning stoves billowing and swirling into the blue sky. The only sign of life on the prairie is a small fox running along the village road that has been cleared of snow by the huge snowplow seen in the distance.

As we trudge through the snow toward our front door at 71F, we are surprised to see a truck approaching. Two fellows are calling out to my husband. "Will, we've been waiting for you. We've got some wood for you. We're your neighbors to give you a hand. You'll need to get the ol' cookstove going." After quick introductions, the three veterans—Will with neighbors John and Pete—have a fire going in the ol' cookstove, turning the frigid shack into a warm one. The woodbox outside the back door is filled with wood; our meager belongings have been brought inside. Before John and Pete leave, they tell us, "Many former war workers of the closed Badger Ordnance Works across Highway 12 are leaving and selling a lot of furnishings and stuff they can't afford to move. There's a bulletin board in the community building. You'll find ads for items you can get at low cost."

Will keeps the fire going in the stove as, together, we are preparing the childrens' beds. We unpack and place a space heater in each bedroom. The most needed item is a bed for our son. He is two and is ready to be out of his crib. As we look around our small bathroom, Will discovers there is no immersion heater on the overhead water tank. There is no hot water for showers or baths. Will is always most innovative. Before long, we have hot water.

He has placed a hot plate, found as we unpack, under the water tank, saying, "This should do till I can replace it with an immersion heater and repair it properly." As we look around, we plan and laugh, knowing we will make some exciting and interesting changes that will create a home for our family to enjoy.

When we visited Badger last year, we met Mr. Lawrence Halle, Manager of Badger Village. He personally greeted us in his office. The administrative office is an extension of residence halls on campus in Madison. When we received our keys to 71F, Mr. Halle assured us that our lease guaranteed maintenance and paint as needed free of charges. He introduced the friendly office employees who sell bus tickets, collect our rent each month, and keep things running well.

Our rent is twenty-seven dollars each month. We have learned that rent is based on the size of the unit and the family size. The rent is less when the need is greater because there are children. How fair! What a blessing!

We have no car, but there are old school buses that go directly to the Madison campus each day and home each evening. God is good.

This is our first Saturday in our hometown. Sauk Prairie covered in snow is so beautiful. It's cold. The sun is shining on the snow, making a pleasant walk as we explore pulling the sled. The kids are having a great time. They are cozy in blankets with caps, mittens and scarves for warmth. We have a small map of our village to help us learn the location of row houses, streets, and the community building in relation to the school and 71F. Because our daughter starts school on Monday, we are exploring that area first of all. Perhaps, if the school is open, we shall be able to locate her room.

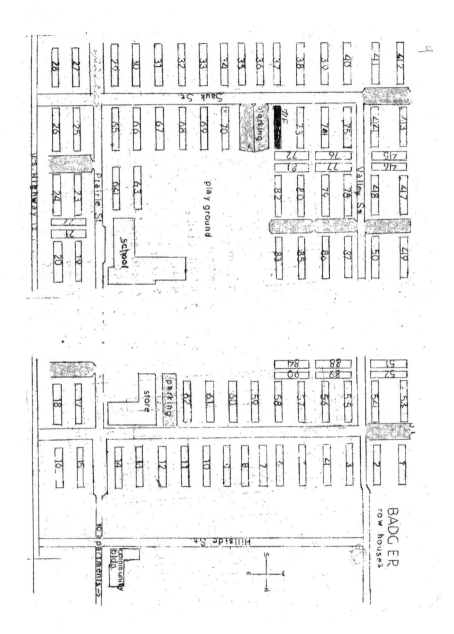

We have discovered a vacant space next door to our unit. We inquire at Mr. Halle's office for approval to move a wall in order to add that space to ours. They have granted our request. We have planned that the best way to get it accomplished is to ask Will's friend Russ. He is a veteran on the GI Bill, is living here in Badger Village, and is here to help. While opening the space, a kitchen with all the shelves and drawers intact and a closet was found and was moved to our third bedroom. We have four feet of space added to the living room. We also have the key and permission to use the remaining space next door.

War workers and their families are leaving Badger and are selling unwanted furniture and items they don't want to move. After searching through the ads on the bulletin board in the community building, we locate a family moving, anxious to sell many items we can use. Luck is with us. For two hundred dollars cash, we have gotten a Victrola (phonograph), a small living room couch, two lamps, bunk beds, a dresser, and a piano. We are told by the father, "We'll deliver all the things you've bought and place the piano, beds, and couch where you want. There are a lot of lads here willing to help. We need to move quickly to where's work. The children will have excellent schools here."

Many families have lived in Badger for years as workers at the Hercules Badger Ordnance Works. The Badger Ordnance Works on Sauk Prairie was built on the most fertile farmland in Wisconsin when the US federal government took 10,565 acres of farms, fields, and land then gave notice to more than eighty farm families to vacate their farms and move in seven weeks. Construction of a sixty-five-million-dollar ($65,000,000.00) munition Hercules Powder Plant was completed on the Wisconsin River.

During World War II, Badger Ordnance City near Sauk City, Wisconsin, on Highway 12, was the housing complex for thousands of families working at Badger Ordnance Works. By the end of the war, the name Badger, Wisconsin, was officially authorized by the United States post office. In 1945, the war department publicized the Badger Ordnance City as surplus.

The Federal Housing Administration received petitions from cities, universities, and colleges across the country, requesting the vacant buildings to not be demolished but moved to their cities or university campuses.

Housing was in short supply all over the country, and housing for veterans with families enrolling in the GI Bill was a high priority for universities in 1945 and 1946. The University of Chicago trucked 125 housing units from Badger, Wisconsin, to its campus. Iowa, Michigan, Minnesota universities, and campuses throughout Wisconsin, including the University of Wisconsin, moved units from Badger.

Administrators from the university visited Badger and made the decision to acquire the whole of Badger from the US government for housing married students and provide buses to take them to the Madison campus. This was the first time in the hundred years as a functioning University in Wisconsin that a provision was made for housing married students and those with children.

In the early days, the now well-known scientist John Muir was one of the earliest resident students in North Hall, the first building for student housing at the university.

We take our daughter to school on Monday, and we are pleased to see the well-equipped, well-staffed, and well-organized school she'll be attending. We meet the principal and Karen's teacher, Ms. Viola Lauring. Ms. Lauring explains, "The classes are for youngsters in kindergarten through eighth." We also are shown the well-planned nursery, which is the first nursery school in the state for children ages two to five. The school construction and the planning in every area—including the library, lighting, desks, and toilets—are excellent.

The staff seem exuberant and well-educated in childcare. Ms. Lauring, the director, has degrees in child welfare and education from the University of Minnesota. She taught three years at Oklahoma A&M College before coming to Badger.

The school and the nursery are the best equipped in the country, financed by the federal government during World War II for families living at Badger working at the Hercules Powder Plant across Highway 12.

We enrolled our wee one of two years in the nursery school for two half days a week to see if he'll enjoy the experience.

Since the children are in school until lunch, we walk through the snow with our sled. We stop at A&P grocery store and restock our groceries. It's a great opportunity to become acquainted with our community. I brought a little map that was given to us on our arrival.

Badger is indeed a village. We note that there's a place where garden tools are available. We decide to look into having a garden when spring arrives. Our Flexible Flyer sled is loaded with our groceries. The box my husband built on the sled is handy and also comfortable for the kids to ride in when pulled through the snow. We are enjoying the crunching sounds of the snow as we walk.

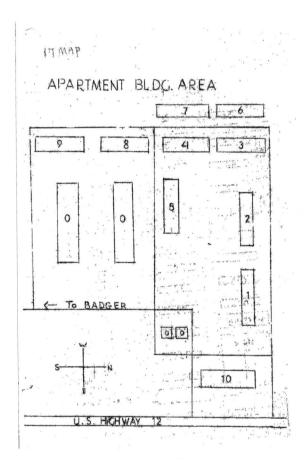

Apartment buildings area

SHOPPING AREA

1 GARDEN TOOLS
2 MAINTENANCE
3 POST OFFICE
4 BARBER
5 TRADING POST
6 DRUG STORE
7 A & P

Shopping area

Will has his good old army boots on. He says, "These will last a long time. These boots took me many miles in the mountains of Italy." It feels so good to be walking, planning, dreaming, laughing, and singing together. What a happy day together! We have a whole week together before his classes and work commitments and bus rides in the old school buses begin. We put away the groceries and place the milk in the icebox, happy to have gotten ice on Saturday from the iceman. I need to learn how long that big block of ice will last in a place next to the wood-burning stove. The wood seems to burn so fast. There's so much to learn.

We warm blankets to put on the sled cause it's time to collect the children. There will be no school for a week. That means we'll play in the snow, make snowmen, build a fort, and take the kids out on the Flexible Flyer. We'll have fun being a family together again—have lots of stories, lots of quiet time together, and lots of popcorn and circus breakfasts!

The year has been a good one; we celebrated birthdays and holidays and learned how to cope without a car, refrigerator, washer, drier, and a host of other "essentials." There has been no burden of having expectations. We have more love than money, and we have faith in God's plan for us.

1947

We attend church each Sunday, and we make time to attend community meetings to meet our neighbors and learn how our village government is organized. Our daughter Karen will have her seventh birthday on January 29. I am determined to learn how to bake a birthday cake and cupcakes using the oven of the old wood cookstove. It should be fun if the stove works as well as my mother's and grandmother's stoves worked. We'll decorate the cake and cupcakes so Karen can take decorated cupcakes to school and also have a birthday party here in our new home. This year is starting great!

During the community meeting, we learn that there is a council, a housing office with Mr. Lawrence Halle (whom we have met), a policeman, a doctor, a transportation supervisor, and a university union consultant. A small booklet *Life at Badger* is provided as a handy reference. It has information regarding open hours of the A&P supermarket, where and how to register for a post office box, bus schedules, information on the trading post, drugstore, barbershop, a short history of Badger, and church services. There are pages titled "Social Life at Badger" outlining the university's union programs and a consultant's role in using the allotted nine-hundred-dollar budget to provide concerts, lectures, cinemas, and dances for adults and programs, parties, festivals, and special celebrations for families.

Badger Village Council is composed of twenty-nine members elected by the Badger Association—residents who have signed leases with the university. Three council members are elected from each ward in South Badger and one from each of the barracks in North Badger to hold office for one year. Wards are numbered I through VI with an approximation of fifteen units in each ward. Our ward is ward V and has units 61 through 75, ours being 71. There are numerous committees and a Badger Wives Club. Every student-wife is welcomed as a member.

The first time I attended a meeting, I was elected to be chairman of ward V. Looks like I'll be busy helping plan a Valentine's Day party for the children, a Valentine dance in February for adults, a St. Patrick's dance, an Easter egg hunt, and events yet to be announced.

The first priority for us is Karen's seventh birthday on January 29. Our house is decorated with balloons, paper cutouts, and garlands. The birthday cake and cupcakes baked in the old cookstove oven turned out well. She has invited six girls from her class in school and Sunday school class to her party. We are busy wrapping presents, including a new game, a book, records, and a new dress we picked out together when we went shopping on a mother-and-daughter fun day. She asked, "Mama, will you wrap it for my birthday?"

I have finally planned the curtains for the kitchen window. Among the things I found in one of the boxes we moved here with is some cotton material. There's a small amount of red, yellow, blue, and white. I can cut into strips and sew together to end up with colorful kitchen curtains. Painting the kitchen with the paint—to which I have added lots of white —will go nicely with the kitchen cupboards I painted.

The next big project is painting the living room and bedroom after moving the wall. I keep praying that I'll think of a way to help with our finances.

Will has gotten two jobs at the university to supplement the ninety dollars, the GI Bill pays him each month. He works and studies long hours, takes the earliest bus in the morning, and comes home late on the last, at ten. With the preschool and nursery school so excellent and available for the wee one's half days, there must be some way I can help with our finances. I must admit, I've a new talent: handling the old cookstove like my grandmother! Gardening and canning like our mothers did is what everyone is talking about. Here we are in the heart of Wisconsin's choicest farmland, and the university is furnishing communal garden tools and marking off plots. A near farmer will prepare ours for planting. Our plot will be at least thirty by sixty feet.

The university plans to bring professors and teachers to help us learn gardening, harvesting, and canning. They will also advise us on the equipment we'll need for canning safely. We are sending off for seed catalogs and deciding what to plant. Since this is a family project, we all agree, "Let's plant our own popcorn." It's all very exciting as we watch snow melt and spring arrive at last!

One day, as I was walking home from the A&P store, my stadium boots were getting so wet and heavy. I kept trying to avoid the melting snow. The purple and white crocuses had popped their heads out of their snow beds. I stopped to admire them and suddenly danced about foolishly feeling spring.

When shopping, splurging is not the usual activity, but I hurried back to the store. Only moments before, I had seen the frozen food counter freshly stocked. The frozen peaches brought to mind the thought of a freshly baked peach cobbler. I couldn't get it out of my mind. I mused

"Can I splurge like this?" half aloud as I picked up a package, took it to the counter, and paid. All the way home, I keep seeing signs of spring, but the wind blowing from the north is cold and makes me hurry to get home. The children help unpack the groceries, and there are shouts of joy as they discover favorite cereals and surprises. There is a flurry of putting away groceries and of getting pots, pans, flour, and everything needed for making the best peach cobbler. Children are begging, "Just one little taste, Mama." I look at the small package and declare, "Not a taste until dessert." This cobbler has gotten quite a buildup, and I intend to serve it as a French chef in his flame room. The smell of baking wafts through my mind as we open the package. A sharp knife has been handed to me by the child not allowed to touch sharp knives.

When the box is cut open at last, there before us are beautiful peaches, layer upon layer of beautiful peaches, and there in the very middle of the top layer of the golden peaches is a beautiful honeybee. No one says a word; we just stand there looking at that honeybee.

When dinner is over, I decide to sit down and write to the company that very evening. I am disappointed and unhappy. I write a letter—no, two—but they end up in the wastebasket. The more I thought about that beautiful honeybee and the wonderment on the faces of my children. I couldn't be cross or disappointed. I find myself composing little verses and laughing at them as I do my chores each day. The next week, I sit down once again, and this time, I write to the president of the company. I have forgotten to ask for a refund or another box of frozen peaches. I simply write the following:

> Your frozen peaches are sweet as honey
> But I didn't expect a bee for my money

Things are going on in the same unpredictable fashion. A glass of milk has just been spilled at dinner, and I am getting it cleaned up when there is a knock on our back door. We have no doorbells at Badger. My husband opens the door. There stands a handsome young man who introduces himself as a representative of Libby, McNeill & Libby of Chicago. "I'm here in response to a message your wife sent to our firm," he says.

He smiles then continues. "I am here to express personal regrets from the president of our firm. He is anxious for you to know that your poem was well received, and he would like to show his appreciation for the unique manner in which the complaint was made. I have left an order at the A&P grocery store here in the village to give you, with our compliments, any frozen food you choose from the case up to fifty dollars. Your poem delighted many people this past week." At this point, he notes we have an icebox—no freezer—and adds, "I'll arrange your purchases to be over a period of time, not all at once if that will work better for you." We shake hands, we thanked him, and when he left, we hug and thank the Lord. I promise I'll make a peach cobbler and let everyone taste the frozen peaches as we open the packages.

University professors with student-helpers are here in our community center to advise these potential canners on the kind of equipment needed. We have invested in a huge water bath canner and a twenty-quart pressure cooker. We are learning their use and which vegetables and fruits are canned safely in each type of canner. This time we spend learning gives us confidence that this new challenge of planting, harvesting, canning, and preserving will be a worthy enterprise.

Very close to Badger Village is a pea and corn cannery. Veteran families are advised that we can purchase cans of peas and corn at discounted prices. We'll skip planting peas and corn. We'll plant sweet corn for corn on the cob and popcorn for popping.

We hear that owners of cherry orchards invite people to come to pick cherries when the cherries are ripe. They say, "Bring your own containers and your family." At the right time, we heard that the cherries are ripe.

We went on a Saturday, took the children, and had a lot of fun. However, to pick, wash, destem, and pit fresh cherries is a nightmare. A huge pail of cherries took two days to prepare for canning. The end result: only five pints of cherries for pie and cobbler.

Fortuitously, I read an article in the Sunday paper about the cherries in Door County, Wisconsin. One can order a thirty-pound tin of frozen, pitted cherries delivered to one's door for a few dollars. I telephoned my order on the community center's phone to arrive COD. We thawed and canned them, and we put twenty-five pints of cherries on our shelves for pies and cobbler.

Our garden plot has been plowed and disked by a neighbor farmer. Soil has been staked out, ready for the seeds we are planting. The red potatoes have been cut, strings on poles have been placed where green beans will be. Corn for corn on the cob and popcorn have already been planted. We have also planted cucumbers and dill for pickles, carrots, radishes, lettuce, and cabbage. Peanuts and tomatoes will go in later.

Rosemary, basil, and other herbs are planted closer to our back door. When we hike into the open fields near our garden, we discover raspberry bushes. We'll gather the raspberries later when they have ripened for jam and syrup.

Will works so hard. He has two jobs at the university. He is a Polio Fellow and is learning about the immune system through his research for a vaccine to end polio. He tells me, "The most interesting classes in medical school are the ones on the immune system and infectious diseases. My degrees in Bacteriology and Microbiology will be helpful. I'd like to pursue a degree in Immunology. I think it's the future of medicine." His research is so very interesting, yet he finds time for family and is always helpful and innovative. At the moment, he is talking with a neighbor who has an oil heater to keep his family warm in winter. Will would like to get one for us.

Our friend Russ comes by and suggests he and Will drive over to where the old farm houses were, across Highway 12. They hope to find flower bulbs and plants that can be transplanted to our yards. They dug up iris, tulip, and various other bulbs and plants. Some lumber to build shelves for canned goods in the closet recently added to our home from next door was found.

They built a lovely window box for our front window. I painted it red and I shall add Norwegian rosemaling. When they are at the old farm houses, Will finds what he thinks is a lilac bush. He transplants it at the end of our house. When it blooms, we'll know by the fragrance of the blossoms if it's a lilac bush.

The activities at Badger Village include dances with an orchestra made up of local musicians called The Collegians. Everyone agrees to plan dances often. We have such a romantic time dancing as couples—sweethearts again.

We have movies—twelve cents for children, thirty cents for adults—square dances, lectures, arts, crafts, and foreign films.

The wives club meetings are fun. Bridge is available, there are excellent speakers, and interesting programs are provided.

I am surprised and honored to be elected chairman of the Badger Wives Club. My experience as chairman of ward V made me aware of the talent among us, and of residents willing to work on committees. We'll have fun producing colorful festivities, picnics, dances, and memorable events, including shows.

I have just learned that a new playground with fences to provide a safe place for children has been requested. At the wives club meeting this evening, I bring it up as our immediate project. There are almost a hundred women present, and everyone votes yes. Committees are formed, and we'll have a worthy project completed successfully this very month. Our Bridge Club also approved the purchase of useful household items as prizes rather than personal cosmetics, perfumes, or purses.

We are a community of caring people, and we share ideas and volunteer to get things done. When I announce that rewiring of electrical lines is being done in order to provide new water heaters, a cheer of gratitude and joy comes forth. I note, however, that no electric stoves can be accommodated on the new electrical circuits.

More than thirty volunteers have come forward when help is requested to get a summer recreation program for the youth of our community underway. The president of our town council, John Smith; chairman of the wives club, Audrey Fahlberg; Reverend Peterson; Ms. Lauring, director of the school; and the university have agreed that this is a first priority since school vacation begins in three weeks. Before our wives club meeting adjourns, I announce, "We have located a mimeograph at the old munition plant office across the highway. This means we can print the Badger Bulletin right here. Trips to the Madison campus to print it will no longer be necessary. We'll need volunteers to print and deliver the bulletin to each ward every Friday."

Spring is here. Easter egg hunt and the St. Patrick dance have become memories as we plan our first formal dance party for April 26. We are having a reception for the president of the university and his wife, and are looking forward to Mr. and Mrs. Fred coming. Everyone is making sure all will go well so our guests will be impressed with Badger Village when they arrive on April 20.

This is a busy time; there are so many family needs and so many commitments. Wouldn't you know, at this moment, I see an ad in a local paper that interests me. The ad reads, "Bookstore in Baraboo closing—children's books for sale, See Jenifer at Bookstore on Saturday if interested." I have told Will, shared with him my ideas, and asked if he will be home Saturday morning so I can go and check it out.

At 9:00 a.m. on Saturday, I am on a bus on my way to Baraboo to meet Jenifer at the bookstore. I was thinking, *Could selling children's books be a business in our village?* I intended to buy a few books only, but Jenifer made an offer to sell the 122 children's books she had left for one dollar each. I bought all of them.

"I have two fifty-dollar bills with me, and I'll take them all if you will accept and trust me for a twenty-two-dollar IOU." We like each other as soon as we meet this morning. She makes an invoice that we both signed, packs the books in big boxes, then we laugh as I say, "How on earth can we get these heavy boxes on the bus?" Jenifer looks at me and says, "No problem. I'll drive you home." As we are leaving, I notice in a corner by the door a stack of old *New Yorker* magazines and ask about them. She says, "They are there for the trash pickup on Monday." I ask, "May I have the covers of all of them?" As we start taking the covers off every magazine, she asks, "What the heck are you needing them for?"

I can see that organizing a book business and finishing my term as Badger Wives Club chairman before garden work and canning begins will take time away from family unless I'm careful. Family has always been my first priority and shall always be. I look forward to the gardening as a family fun time in the country. This location is truly special and beautiful. After church and Sunday school, we walk past the barbershop. I had seen a platform at the front window. Perhaps I could arrange with the barber to display my books for sale there. I have noted that his hours are 7:30 a.m. until 8:30 p.m. Monday to Saturday.

I'll make a point of speaking with the barber this coming week. The Badger Bulletin may be the place to advertise. As we go through the boxes of books, Will agrees that they are excellent books I got at a great bargain. There's a lot of interest, enthusiasm, and fun tonight as we go through the books. We let each child pick one to keep to add to their own book collection and one to read tonight before bedtime.

Everyone is curious about the box of the *New Yorker* magazine covers. I'm telling them that my plan is for us to cover the wall in the bathroom. We'll trim them, paste them on the wall like wallpapering then shellac the wall when the pasted covers are dry. We'll make it a family project. Karen wants to trim the covers and help paste, young Will can help paste, and Daddy can study at the kitchen table close to us in case help is needed. We'll get started next week.

On Monday, my meeting with the barber went well. His platform at the window is a perfect place to display the books. And he is pleased that I offered to pay him, but he refuses and says, "No, indeed, I'd never think of it." We work out all the details and agree I'd have a colorful sign to go along with the display. I'll have each book priced and will need a box for cash. Payment will be on the honor system. In this community, it will work. It's interesting that we agreed the display should be limited to no more than fifteen books at a time. We'll keep it simple.

An artist friend does a great-looking ad for the Badger Bulletin and says, "I'll do one of a child reading a book for your display in the window." How grateful I am for the help.

A lot of time has been spent pricing each book, doing inventory, setting up a ledger, and pulling together all the elements needed for a colorful display in the barbershop window.

I use the time to complete the preparations when children are in school and Will is at the university. It doesn't interfere with family time.

As I am cleaning my son's bedroom today, I take notice of the Playskool puzzles and toys and which ones had been in use for years. The toys are beautifully put together and are colorful. They also help children learn skills.

Badger has more children added to the population each year than any town in Wisconsin. I'm thinking I should contact the company to ask if they would grant me a franchise to sell Playskool toys and to purchase the toys at wholesale prices. I have no telephone. I shall write a letter for information. Wouldn't it be good to have books and toys before Christmas? The books project has been successful. The first week, I was able to pay the IOU to Jenifer and put the two fifty-dollar bills away for my sewing machine savings. The letter to Playskool has been mailed. This will be a slow process; it takes time to send and receive mail, but I have started the process.

We are collecting sweet corn from our very own garden to eat as corn on the cob. The children are running back and forth between the garden and wagon in which I have placed two baskets for them to fill. The carrots, onions, radishes, and lettuce have filled the baskets. Our three-year-old keeps saying, "This is fun work, Mama." We laugh and sing and agree it is fun work.

The canning has begun. The tomatoes, onions, and spices combined with ground beef became jars of excellent spaghetti sauce. We also are canning vegetables for soup. The kitchen is a busy place. The smell of all these special combinations and the sight of the completed jars cooling make us so grateful.

Will and I do the canning at night. He comes home on an earlier bus when we have canning. The huge hot water bath canner, when filled with boiling water, is heavy to handle, and the twenty-quart pressure cooker, when filled with full jars, is heavy and can be dangerous. The pressure gauge must be carefully watched. Because of all the hot water and other dangers apparent in the canning process, we tuck the children safely in their beds with love, stories, and prayers before we begin. The best fun for our family is going to our garden, finding different vegetables ready for harvesting, and watching for birds.

We have been told birds are returning to Badger. During World War II, when the huge munitions plant was in full operation, every bird had disappeared from this area. Today we are thrilled to see and hear meadowlarks, bobolinks, and inland sandpipers. A neighbor told us of seeing red-winged blackbirds. According to the number of rabbits we see and the lettuce we don't see, there should be bunnies. We know they are here.

Letters arrive from Playskool, requesting personal information and my plan for financing. They inform that I shall need a Dun & Bradstreet approval rating. Fortunately, one letter is signed with the name of the person with whom I must speak along with the telephone number.

Here's my opportunity to inform Playskool about the large number of young families at Badger who will purchase toys. Also, I shall need advice and help on how to obtain a Dun & Bradstreet rating. It all sounds absolutely impossible, but I have learned possible just takes a little longer. If it is meant to be, prayers will be answered.

As I wait, I enjoy each day hiking with the children and also to the nearby farmer to get eggs. We enjoy these cool September days, before school starts, exploring, digging our peanuts, harvesting the popcorn, and storing peanuts and popcorn in the room next door to dry before shelling.

We have been given the key to the room next door to use the space as needed. Will has put up clotheslines there, which means I'll not hang clothes outside when winter-weather snow and frigid winds arrive. During September and October, we are finishing the canning. Apple sauce, a lug of peaches, a box of pears, and raspberries have been picked for jam, and syrup. This has added more than a hundred jars to our shelves. We have planned to store all the canning equipment away today.

It's such a beautiful Saturday. We put on sweaters and caps for a nice country hike for family fun instead of work. We decide to stop at our neighbor Joe's farm to get eggs on the way home. Joe asks, "How is the canning going?" My husband says, "It's finished for this year. Our garden project and harvest was more successful than we dreamed. We have over five hundred jars canned—mostly garden produce."

"Have you ever canned chicken?" our neighbor Joe asks.

Will says "never" rather emphatically.

We are invited by the farmer's wife, Dorothy, to go to their basement to see the canned chicken they had just finished. Frankly, I'm very impressed and interested, especially when they offered to sell us ten chickens for thirteen cents a pound. They offer to cut off the heads and put the chickens in a big bag so we can get them home.

After church the next day, we take turns playing and reading with the kids and plucking feathers off, washing, and preparing chickens for canning. After cutting them up, I put them in our icebox until Monday. When Will leaves for the university and while the children are in school, I'll can those chickens now that I am an experienced canner.

We'll have chicken and dumplings for dinner tonight to celebrate our successful garden and gleaning. As a surprise, I pick up two packages of frozen peaches from the A&P. Tomorrow after school, we'll taste those peaches and make a peach cobbler together as I had promised.

I also pick up the mail. There's a letter from Playskool that I'll read tonight while Will studies. Tonight we are playing old maid and other games and are having popcorn and a Tut and Tootles story before prayers and bedtime.

As I sit down to catch my breath, I realize Thanksgiving is almost here, then Christmas, and before that, young Will's third birthday on December 8. Will and I have been wondering what we can do to make it special for such an active little tyke as our son.

At last, I have had the courage to open the letter from Playskool. I'm hesitant even though the many conversations with the gentleman at Playskool have made me hopeful and expectant. They liked and approved the information I have sent them. Fortunately, I was truthful about our finances and my plans for a great success because of all the families with children. Prayers have been answered.

No franchise is needed, and Dun & Bradstreet has approved my application. I have gotten a Dun & Bradstreet rating! I'm told that a shipment of toys and puzzles along with a small display rack is being delivered to our address. These are all samples. The invoice shows, "Balance due: zero (0) dollars." The next shipments will show wholesale cost on all toys and should arrive before Christmas. I am so blessed that I was able to give such excellent references on my papers provided. Thank you, Heavenly Father.

Will and I are sharing such joy. We are expecting our third child in mid-June of 1948. This family increase means no gardening and canning next year. We are blessed! Will is doing so well with the management of his time. He's at the highest level of all his medical classes and his research. He's a Polio Fellow trying to discover a vaccine for polio and is getting more interested in the immune system as he studies. He tries to spend time with us each week.

At this time, he and a neighbor are installing an oil heater. The neighbor who is moving from Badger has just given it to us. The oil tank fits perfectly inside the woodbox outside the back door, just as it fitted in the neighbor's. The heater will replace the old wood heater in the kitchen. The neighbors have been war workers and lived in Badger many years.

They suggested we take their "used but reliable" refrigerator off their hands also. The day the refrigerator arrives and before the old icebox is taken away, Karen and I take the big drip pan from it. We make a beautiful terrarium for her pet turtle. He seems very happy on the sand among the rocks and plants Karen has arranged for him. The terrarium has been painted and looks very nice on the shelf. Moving the wall gave shelves for her books, records, treasures, drawers, and space for her turtle's terrarium.

We told our families we will have Thanksgiving here in Badger—our new home. So here we are; our little family is having a delightful Thanksgiving dinner selected from our larder of over five hundred jars of food we have harvested, canned, and preserved. Our Victrola has soft music playing. The oil heater keeps us warm and cozy as we watch the blizzard dump piles of snow outside our windows. There will be snowmen, snowballs, forts, and angel wings in the snow tomorrow—lots of fun and lots of wet mittens! The big snow plow is out in the blizzard. The powerful light has gotten young Will's attention. We have given him permission to leave the dinner table and run to the window to watch as it passes our home. Later when we are having a quiet time, Will says into my ear, "Honey, let's find out if a ride in that huge snow plow can be arranged for his birthday on December 8." I said "great idea" as quietly as I could.

It is special, and it's the eventful time we hear about over and over in great detail. Christmas is a wonderful time of the year. We are baking a birthday cake to celebrate the birthday of Jesus. Cookies are being rolled out and decorated before baking. The kiddos are helping. It's messy but fun. Our little village is a winter wonderland of snow.

There are lots of parties for children and adults. A Christmas break from school is welcome. Will has special time at home getting time with family and some needed rest. At the moment, he and his son are building a little radio from spare parts they found among young Will's collection. At three years of age, it's amazing the talent he has for collecting and creating all sorts of objects.

A break from having to ride the old school bus for a few days is a gift for Will. He enjoys the time with his daughter, playing card games, working on puzzles and art projects. They read poetry and sometimes make up stories. She will be eight soon.

1948

New Year has arrived. Plans for the New Year festivities are underway. There will be a dance on New Year's Eve and parties and special events at the community center for the whole village.

We are planning a birthday party on January 29 for Karen's eighth birthday, and we are making invitations she will give to her school friends. At last, after much anticipation, six friends arrive, each with a gift in hand. Little girls partying sound so happy. After playing games, listening to some records, singing, playing the piano, and dancing, they sing "Happy Birthday, Karen" as she blows out the eight candles, on her decorated cake. They are enjoying cake and ice cream as I listen to all the excitement of Karen opening presents.

Sorting out coats, caps, scarves, mittens, galoshes, and boots by the front door before the girls go out into the snow and cold air is not a problem. It's all part of the fun and laughter. Karen gives me a big hug. "Thanks, Mama, for the party and all those cupcakes you brought to school yesterday." What a loving way to end the party, then we celebrate together as she opens the surprise gifts we have for her. We sing "Happy Birthday" as she blows out the candles on leftover cake we are sharing. Karen says, "It's so fun to be eight."

We are filled with joy because by the middle of June, we'll welcome a new baby into our family. Our three children will be about four years apart. I'll have such pleasure nurturing a new child. This big family event will bring a change for all of us. We certainly will not want to tend to a big garden or do canning. Maybe some berry picking, watching for birds and bunnies, trips on the bus to Madison to the doctor, and visiting Grandma Vera and Grandpa in Madison.

Valentines are being made from red construction paper, ribbons, paper doilies, and trimmings I've collected. We make our own paste from flour and water, which becomes part of the messy fun. The valentine for Daddy is the most decorative. There are some for teachers and friends. Then there's one with whispered secrets taking place. Maybe for Mom? Valentine's Day is here, and so much caring and loving create a happy time at school for the children as well as at home. Little gifts are exchanged. I receive a lovely potted plant and a box of fine chocolates from Will and the children. Happy time!

The first of March, I was asked to write a story about Badger Village for the newspaper the *Wisconsin State Journal*. I got busy right away in putting together an article entitled "Badger Village," which was published in the Sunday paper on March 7, 1948.

The article was well received. Enclosed are copies of letters which I appreciated receiving. I have included a photo of our children—Karen, eight years, and Willson Jr., soon four—and their pregnant mother.

St. Patrick's Day was all about wearing green, parties, green-frosted shamrock cookies for the kiddos, a big dance for all sweethearts, and the local musicians, the Collegians, playing their hearts out while everyone sang those old Irish favorites. We danced and sang for an hour and continued singing as we walked home. Together, we were planning for our big event in June: the new addition to our sweet family. The flowers Will and Russ dug and moved from the old farms across Highway 12 to our window boxes are blooming. The peonies, lilies, iris, and daisies are showing signs of blooms. We are watching the lilac bushes, hopeful we'll have the fragrance of lilacs to enjoy.

We'll have flowers to tend and a new baby and children to nurture rather than a garden this summer. Our whole family is talking about our baby's birth in June.

For Mother's Day on Sunday, May 9, we have invited our family to Badger Village to have dinner in our community center's dining room and to see our new home. We have two birthdays to celebrate along with Mother's Day. My sister Lenore Johnson and my nephew Randy Habeck will have birthdays. When twenty or more Norwegians get together and each family brings food to share, there will be plenty of food and laughter. I am always reminded I have thirty-seven cousins and twenty aunts and uncles. Many are here today, and upon leaving, I was pleasantly surprised with a baby shower they have planned.

Our family is spending the evening unwrapping gifts and placing the small items in the dresser, which we painted white to match the crib in our bedroom. Today at our gathering, we shared a Playskool toy with each child under six years. I let each child pick a favorite. Each one of the older children left with a book.

The end of the school year is approaching, and vacation will be a time for fun and games for all the kids at Badger. The well-planned programs include swimming, sports for all ages, games, art, music, and crafts. Adults have graciously volunteered to share their time and expertise. Our children are enrolled.

Will and I have some serious planning for the middle of June. The children will stay with Grandma Vera and Grandpa in Madison. My doctor is in Madison, and the delivery will be at Madison General Hospital. Will can continue his research as a Polio Fellow at the university while I'm in the hospital. Diapers are washed. The crib is newly painted with a new mattress, and the quilts, blankets, and sheets given to us at the shower are ready. The doctor tells us to "plan on being here by June 15." Everyone has a small bag with essentials packed. Will has decided to sleep at his parents' home with the kids. His parents are so pleased to be a part of welcoming a new grandchild.

Our friend Russ is driving us to Madison on June 15 as the doctor suggested, and by late afternoon, after getting the children settled, Russ is driving us to the hospital. Things are coming together. We hug Russ as he leaves for Badger.

The sixteenth of June comes and goes. We pray together. Will sings quietly to me as nurses keep checking. Time moves on. Midnight turns to June 17. At 2:30 a.m., a beautiful tiny baby girl with blue eyes and blond curls who weighs six and a half pounds is placed in my arms. When she comes to my breast, I discover she is born with two baby teeth. The nurse arrives with a nipple shield. Will is right beside me with a hug and a loving kiss and open arms. The nurse places his baby daughter in his arms and tells him, "We have a cot ready for you to spend the night." It is comforting to have him close and to know he didn't walk home or have to get a taxi at three thirty in the morning. Later in the day, happiness is the sound of voices as family arrives with flowers and kisses to meet their new baby sister. Daddy looks proud and happy! Five days have passed, and Russ is here to take us home.

The month of July has arrived. It's my birthday on July 1. We are having a big party. There's a birthday cake decorated. Candles are lighted.

Cards and small gifts have been wrapped. I make a big wish as I have help blowing out the candles.

On the twentieth of July, we make a chocolate cake with mint frosting decorated by the kids for Daddy. Little gifts and handmade cards are on the table for him as he blows out the candles while we all sing "Happy Birthday."

Then on July 30, we celebrate our wedding anniversary. We celebrated all summer, including July 4!

One of our neighbors gives us a baby buggy that is like new and can be converted to a stroller. It works great on our sidewalks. The fun and games, swim classes, tennis, dance classes, arts and crafts, and all the fun of summer has changed to school starting in September. Fall, winter, Halloween, Thanksgiving, and Christmas. Time moves on.

December 8 will be young Will's birthday. He'll be four. Remembering how much he enjoyed the snowplow ride when he was three, we plan to arrange it again.

Will's days are full. He has daily rides on the old school buses to the university—early mornings, late nights home, and studying at all hours. He also has work as well as his research as a Polio Fellow. How he is able to have the highest grades possible, work on the vaccine for poliomyelitis research project, take so many credits in each semester, hold two jobs at the university, have time for family, and keep his delightful personality and sense of humor intact, I'll never know!

As for me, I am busy with the children, and I'm helping by being organized and having a happy home, good meals, full cookie jar—no canning this year. The Playskool project is going well; the children are healthy, smart, and delightful. Today I'm making sure everyone's winter clothes are ready. It's predicted that big snow storms are coming this way.

We'll be watching for the giant snowplow on our street like we did last year. We have arranged for young Will's birthday surprise on December 8.

On December 8, we wake up to a winter wonderland. Buses to the university are cancelled. We'll have a birthday breakfast of circus pancakes and cinnamon-toast soldiers. Daddy has his apron ready. We sing "Happy Birthday" to young Will as he sits at the table, ready for our family circus breakfast. He doesn't know about the big surprise we have arranged with the snowplow driver to blow the horn when he comes on our street. The snow keeps coming all through the day.

As late afternoon comes, I say, "Let's get warm winter coats, caps, and mittens by the door so we can see the snowplow when it comes around." We are getting into our warmest winter clothes and galoshes when we hear the loud horn. Everyone shouts "Here he comes! He's on our street!" as we open the door and hurry out. It's dark, and the huge lights are shining on the snow. Instead of waving and driving past, he stops. He calls to young Will, "Come on, birthday boy, let your daddy lift you up for a ride around the village. We'll take your daddy along to keep us company." They climb on, settle into the big seat next to the driver, and off they go.

Karen and I wave and hurry into the house to check on the sleeping baby. We'll have popcorn, Kool-Aid, and birthday cake with the candles ready, and wait at the window till we see the big lights of the snowplow so we can have the door open for the guys when they get here. It is such a happy family time. We all listen as a bright-eyed four-year-old tells us in detail how a big snowplow operates. We unwrap lots of little gifts, and bring out a Playskool puzzle and toys. After we blow out candles and sing "Happy Birthday" and "Let It Snow" as well as other tunes, a little girl wakes up and joins the fun. A happy four-year-old is sharing hugs and kisses with his two sisters, his mama, and his daddy. We sing together.

Christmas is coming, geese are getting fat.

Pleased to put a penny in an old man's hat.

If you haven't got a penny, a half penny 'il do.

If you haven't got a half penny, God bless you.

We are excited about Christmas for the kids. We have just learned from a neighbor that they are moving and want to sell a little portable record player (in new condition). They have records their children have outgrown. For ten dollars, it is truly a bargain. We go to their apartment, look it over carefully, and play a couple of the forty-five records that are for children of all ages. There will be records to separate by age. The children will have their own collection.

Today Will is making a stand for our Christmas tree. After church, we put on our warmest clothes. On the Flexible Flyer sled, we bundled the two youngest, we held Karen's hand, and we went to find a small Christmas tree. The snow was deep; no trees were close by. We ended up at the A&P store, where we found a small one exactly the kind we can afford. It is perfect to enjoy in our small living room.

After dinner, we are cutting and pasting some white wrapping paper into snowflakes and are coloring and designing decorations from tinsel and ornaments I have saved from last Christmas. Karen suggests, "Mama, let's make garlands of popcorn for our tree and some to eat now."

We all shouted yes. We get started popping our garden popcorn that was dried and shelled and is disappearing. We may have to plant some next year. It was and still is so good. There are Christmas parties for the youngsters, a Christmas dance for adults, and a beautiful tree at the decorated community center for Badger because of the generosity of the university and willing residents who volunteered time and talent.

The baby is such a joy as she grows and learns new ways to entertain us. She giggles and laughs at the antics of her big brother and claps her hands and makes a singing sound as Karen hugs her and sings to her.

She gets very happy when they come home from school to play with her. The high chair is in use again. I am so glad we saved it. Meril enjoys sitting in it and keeps me company when I'm busy in the kitchen and when everyone is gone. She enjoys the homegrown vegetables I mash and strain, and she tries to eat the cereal with her little silver spoon while getting it mostly on her hands and face. Our family enjoys this precious addition to our lives. Christmas vacation is almost over and a new year will begin. We are staying home to play games, have stories, sing along to the Christmas records we have playing on our Victrola, and dance and celebrate New Year's Eve with our children instead of dancing at the community center party.

1949

❧❦❧

The snowplow continues its rounds through the village. As he comes on our street, he adds snow to the snow fort we are building in our yard. We'll be cozy and warm tonight as we appreciate the heat generated by the oil heater, remembering the old woodstove that had to be stoked up to prevent it from going out before wood was brought in from the woodbox outside in the freezing winter weather.

We are enjoying our storage of canned goods in our larder, especially the chicken. We have plenty of pickles, jam, and syrup as well as cherries, fruits and vegetables to last all winter. We often laugh at recalling the cherry picking.

We also get a kick out of remembering the chicken canning project. When the weather clears a bit and the sun is shining, we'll take our trusty Flexible Flyer sled, bundle up the baby, and visit our farmer friends. We are almost out of eggs.

The family has gotten back into our routine of school after the holidays. Daddy leaves on the early bus each morning and returns on the late bus. He has so many obligations: he manages to be at the top of his medical classes, takes double the required number of hours, holds two jobs, researches, as a Polio Fellow, plus has a family! That's my Will!

January is a time for planning some special surprises for Karen for her birthday on January 29. I have located a piano tuner who will come to our home. We want the piano all tuned up and ready for Karen to have piano lessons. Surprise! She has talked about ballet and dance classes a friend in Madison enjoys. Enrolling her in a class means a round-trip bus ride to Madison each Saturday, but the opportunity for her is there. We'll do it! She keeps her Christmas bike in her bedroom awaiting spring. She'll ride it on our sidewalk, when cleared of snow.

I am sewing a new red jacket for her on my new Singer sewing machine. On the pockets, I'm embroidering flowers. I thank the Lord for all the blessings. Our love is the glue that holds our life together, and our beautiful children are gifts of love. We are grateful. We are enjoying our children. We are a happy family making memories, watching each one grow in grace, having joy, laughing, and learning. Will has a big load in medical school—more than the previous year. His immunology medical classes keep him studying more and later each night. The immune system is like discovering a new world in medicine, and he is part of it now. His plan is to become an immunologist. He tells me, "Audsie, we must find a vaccine for polio! I appreciate and know your love and caring acceptance of my long days away and hours at night studying. My research as a Polio Fellow is an honor, and there is so much work to be done before a vaccine emerges. Many people are engaged in this research project, sharing results and ideas as we continue to communicate across the country. Having my degree in bacteriology, master in microbiology and infectious disease study is helpful." I am so grateful and proud of my husband and father of our children. We all love him.

When the weather is pleasant, we hike. Birds are everywhere. Quite by serendipity, we discover a mockingbird's nest in the lilac bush Will had planted right after moving here. The flowers planted at the same time are happy.

I am busy sewing a lovely ballet costume for Karen. Her dance recital in Madison will be soon, and we all are looking forward to attending with great anticipation. She is going to be a beautiful, lovely ballerina. She has big blue eyes and blond hair and is very smart and always enjoys learning. A new school year will begin soon, and young Will starts kindergarten. He knows numbers and can read. He will like school as his sister does. When I finish Karen's ballet costume, I plan to sew some new shirts for him and a dress for Karen.

We look forward to weekends. Sunday comes, and here we are, mother and children at the kitchen table eagerly awaiting the Sunday surprise. Father with his apron on is working over the old cookstove and toaster, preparing circus pancakes and cinnamon-toast soldiers. Smiles, clapping hands, signs of polite expectation as if it's a first time experience. Each plate arrives with a circus parade of many-colored pancakes and lovingly designed cinnamon toast soldiers marching around the plate. We hold hands for the blessings then dig in. When it's time to clear away the traveling show of imagined circus, we all pitch in. It's church time.

The Playskool toy business is a great success and is providing extra money. The barber is happy to have the display of colorful toys just as he had been pleased to have the books. He tells me that his children enjoy the toys I have given as much as they enjoy the books I gave when he was so kind to offer the vacant space at his front window. The arrangement we have works well because no money changes hands in the barbershop. There is a place to check the toy number desired and name of customer on an order sheet as part of the toy display. Toys are ordered, and the customer pays me when their toy arrives.

The toys are delivered by Playskool to our door. My neighbor collects the toy and pays me at that time. The neighbor knows the exact amount to pay because each toy displayed is priced. It all works out because we have the space next door to us for our use.

Spring is when every gardener begins to plan and order seed catalogs. The next spring, we have other plans, and there will be no garden and no canning—but for now, we have to plan for another cold winter in Badger. Time seems to go quickly as we watch the children grow taller and family needs are greater. Our dreams are coming closer to reality.

1950

Our days at Badger Village are numbered. Will's medical degrees will be completed and awarded in 1951. In the next year, we'll be giving and selling more than we'll be acquiring. We'll be the family moving away. In the meantime, we are planning what we need to keep. We know the crib can be changed to a youth bed. With a new mattress, sheets, and blankets, it will serve well. Karen's antique bed and the new bedspread and chair cover I made we'll keep and move as well as the bunk beds. We enjoy the old Victrola and the collection of records, but I know the Victrola will be given away or sold.

I'm getting ahead of myself. As our winter is coming again, so soon after September, the children need warmer clothes. They have outgrown the old. Off we go on the bus to Baraboo for a day of shopping. It's quite an adventure, or should I say undertaking? This bus ride into the surrounding hills of Baraboo is very different than the ride to Madison. The baby is on my lap and sees the same things from the window. She is learning new words as we go because she listens to her sister and brother. The bus driver is a jolly man and seems to enjoy the kids. The bus fare is twenty-five cents round trip. Kids ride for free.

I asked our driver, "Can you recommend a store that will have children's winter jackets, coats, caps, mittens, and school clothes?" His reply came with no hesitation. "Yes, and I can drive you to the door. In two hours, I'll be coming to drive you back to Badger Village." This is one example of service provided by the university for veteran families living in Badger Village. Most families do not have cars.

Exactly what is chosen, we have purchased to everyone's delight and need—great colors, perfect sizes. Nineteen fifty is a time with no computers and no credit cards for women in their name. Payment was expected in cash. Will and I had plans to spend about one hundred dollars on each of the two older children, but the total, including a coat and cap for baby, came to $185. I added a brightly colored scarf for each one. Young Will suggested we pick a scarf for Daddy as a surprise. I let him choose one like his. Karen picks out a scarf for her sister, Meril. We all agree the blue one matched her blue eyes. Karen, being nine, had chosen a multicolored scarf very much like one of mine she liked.

Because it's Saturday, we are able to be home by noon. Will has a quiet time all morning to study. After lunch, everyone has rest time. Will went back to studying. After dinner, we had showtime. Showing all the warm clothes was fun and timely; there's wind blowing, and it's snowing. The scarf for Father was a great surprise; he's very happy, so everyone clapped as he paraded around the room showing off.

It's Sunday morning, and we are still in jammies, trying to decide if the snowstorm and the wind are becoming too intense for us to get out in it to walk to church. Through our window, we are watching the snow collecting at our door. Karen suggests, "Let's have a circus breakfast, and Daddy will you tell us a Happy Valley story with Norma the witch and our animal friends, like Tut and Tootles?" Daddy laughs and says, "Looks like it's a unanimous decision, kids. That means we all agree. We'll get dressed and stay at home today together."

The first snowstorm in September usually comes with light snow and no wind. Perhaps the storm today indicates a colder winter and one of the heavier snowstorms. We're glad to have the oil heater and warm winter clothes for the children. When the weather turns really cold, the heavy winter army clothing—including coats, boots, gloves, and caps—are worn by all the veterans to try to keep warm on that unheated old school bus ride to and from the Madison campus. Will plans to spend more time at the university on research and at the library to study on campus. His arrival home will be on the last bus at 10:00 p.m. I'll always have a hot meal, and love waiting for him.

We listen to our phonograph (record player) often. Our collection of records includes Uncle Remus stories, which are fun; Cinderella; Andersen's Fairy Tales; Grimm's Fairy Tales; and *The Camel with the Wrinkled Knees* (a Raggedy Ann and Andy adventure). For quiet times, we have many excellent music records in our collection. We enjoy singing along and listening to them. Books are always available for all ages of our children. *The Real Mother Goose* is a favorite. There's Thumper, Bambi, Peter Rabbit, and all the Raggedy Ann stories: *Raggedy Ann's Wishing Pebble, Marcella: A Raggedy Ann Story, Raggedy Ann's Magical Wishes, Raggedy Ann in Cookie Land*, and *The Paper Dragon: A Raggedy Ann Adventure*. The books about horses by Marguerite Henry, *A Child's Garden of Verses* by Robert Louis Stevenson, Nancy Drew books, Mark Twain books, and many others are in Karen's collection.

This is our last year at Badger Village. We are working with the university, the Red Cross, and our community on projects. I try to help our committees in area V in planning parties or school activities. My family comes before everything; I am less able to participate. No more playing bridge or attending every wives club meeting. There are many ways to be helpful without having to be gone from my home. We are having a family Thanksgiving and a few days together, watching the snow collecting in our front yard. The snowman becomes larger and taller; in fact, Daddy has to reach to put the final touches and the hat on the snowman's head.

Young Will's sixth birthday comes so soon after Thanksgiving. This year, he has invited four of his best friends to a party. They are building a huge snow fort into a drift created overnight by the snowstorm. They are having such fun climbing in and out and on top of it until it all collapsed.

When the snowplow man is making the afternoon run through the village, he stops at our house and invites the five little boys to climb inside. What a great surprise! As they drop their snowy mittens, caps, coats, and boots at the door, I hear them laughing and saying, "This is the best birthday party." Hot chocolate and a birthday cake with lighted candles are ready. Six are blown out as young Will exclaimed, "I made six wishes."

We have a 45 record playing an Uncle Remus story, which the boys are enjoying before getting their warm clothes on. They are all neighbors and live nearby. Each little boy receives a small gift to take home as Willie opens his presents from them. Such fun today! This evening, we light the candles and sing "Happy Birthday" once again. After dinner, the snowplow stops, Willie climbs up by himself and has his special birthday surprise.

Will arrives home on the ten o'clock bus cold and hungry. I was watching at the door for him. While he washed and warmed up, he shared his day and love. After his dinner, he went quietly into each bedroom and gently kissed each one of his children. I assured him, "You'll hear all about his birthday party directly in person on Sunday."

This Christmas is the coldest we remember. The fifty degrees below zero temperature prevents our going to the woods to cut our Christmas tree. We buy one again at the A&P store and find a string of colored lights at a good price. Our collection of decorations includes tinsel, red garlands, children's art, and of course, strings of popcorn—some to eat as well. Christmas vacation time is a true blessing this year. We are warm and cozy and enjoying our oil heater. Will and I pray together often, thanking our Heavenly Father for all the unexpected blessings.

Despite the cold, snowy weather, Christmas parties for adults and children are planned to be held in the community center. Church services are held, and caroling is heard throughout the village. Snowmen on the yards in front of the row houses are everywhere. The welcome sunshine each day is a blessing; therefore, most community events are held during daylight hours. Families walk everywhere, as very few have cars. We are always open to unexpected joy and discoveries, as we are surrounded with serendipitous blessings. The holidays have ended. Time to get back to the schoolwork and plans for a good new year.

1951

January is here. This will be a truly important year for our family because of Will's graduation. The first big event is Karen's eleventh birthday on January 29. She makes lovely invitations, which she will give to four of her best friends to invite them to come to our home for her birthday party. I bake a rainbow cake as she had requested, and it turns out to be so special. We all watch her blow out the lighted candles as we sing "Happy Birthday." The girls have so much fun playing the piano, singing, laughing, dancing, playing games, and listening to records. She receives very nice gifts, and the girls enjoy their little treasures to take home. After they leave, Karen gives me a big hug and says, "Thanks, Mama, for the fun party."

Time is going so quickly. It's hard to believe that our cold, cold winter is over and that spring has arrived. The lilac bush has grown and has shown signs of blooming again. It's the year of Will's graduation, Meril will soon be three, young Will is seven, and Karen is eleven. We are packing our meager precious belongings.

Will has accepted a professorship at Baylor College of Medicine as a Microbiologist/Immunologist in Houston, Texas. He graduates with the highest honors; therefore, he had been offered opportunities by outstanding companies and universities. An important factor when he made a decision is that he can continue his research for a vaccine for polio at Baylor College of Medicine in Houston.

At the moment, we are packing the items that will go with us. Next, we plan to separate out items to be sold or given to neighbors. We plan to travel to Houston by train, and we have reserved a family compartment. Each one of us will carry a small bag with personal essentials, books, and toys or games for the journey. Some personal items and boxes of clothes will go on the train with us. Furniture will be shipped. The Playskool toy business has been brought to a close. The company has sent a congratulatory letter and an unexpected check. The barber tells me he'll miss having the colorful toys in his window. The moment of Will's graduation is near.

We have a big secret. We have purchased a movie camera as a graduation gift for Will. We plan to bring it with us and take pictures of him walking on campus in his cap and gown. The whole family will be there. It is so special. He is graduating with high honors.

Saying goodbye to neighbors and Badger Village friends after these many years of dear friendship is not easy. Leaving is also a time of anticipation. We are spending the next day at my parents' farm to say goodbye to my mother and dad—the kids' grandparents—then back to Will's parents in Madison overnight to give goodbye hugs. We board the train in Madison for the long journey to Houston.

Our compartment on the train is spacious. Everyone has a comfortable berth. As a celebration, we locate the dining car and have our dinner on the train. This is a great new experience for us as a family. On our first night, we watch out our big window as the train moves through small Wisconsin villages. We hear the train whistle at each crossing. Finally a tired family says their prayers, hug and kiss and crawl into those berths and sleep.

Next day, we have a celebration. Meril turns three. We have handmade birthday cards and small gifts for her. The waiter in the dining car brings a cupcake for each one and one with a lighted candle for Meril to blow out. Everyone in the dining car, including the waiters, are singing "Happy Birthday." Meril smiles, claps her hands, and calls out, "Thank you for singing to me." Everyone smiles as we leave.

As we arrive to our compartment, an announcement comes over the loudspeaker. "Attention, attention, listen closely. Our tracks are running along the mighty Mississippi River. Due to the heavy rains the last few days, our specially trained crews are checking ahead and assessing the situation. Do not be alarmed because the train has slowed. Keep calm. You are safe. Good night."

Daddy hugs us and advises, "Let's pray all is well." No one could sleep soundly. We raise the curtain and watch out the window. There is water very near the tracks, and the train slows more. Daddy starts telling a story—one of our favorites. When he is finished, I suggest, "Let's just rest on our berths. We can snuggle down because we'll be on the train most likely all night."

After about half an hour, another announcement comes over the loudspeaker. "Folks, we must go very slowly. We suggest everyone to get sleep. Have the clothes you'll be wearing tomorrow and personal bag you came on the train with close at hand."

We did sleep. I look at my watch and realize it's five in the morning, and everyone is wide awake. We gather at the big window to see water all around us. We are traveling through the flood very slowly now. We are informed that special crews have been working along the tracks ahead of the train, keeping the engineer informed about the condition of the tracks all through the night. We quickly get dressed and get our things all packed as suggested. We watch out on our big window.

Daddy tells us, "We have passed through seven states: Wisconsin, Illinois, Missouri, Kentucky, Tennessee, and Mississippi. Now we'll be crossing the mighty Mississippi River into Louisiana."

We are asked to leave everything in our compartment except the small bags we brought on with our essentials. All luggage and sealed boxes must be left in our compartment. It can be collected in two days in Houston at the train station. We will be served a complimentary breakfast now in the dining car. The train makes its way through the flooded world we see through the window. As we arrive in Louisiana, we are told "Everyone must leave the train." We hold hands and leave the train to get on the bus that will take us to Houston, Texas.

We have learned our train was the last one to get through the flood safely. We arrive in Houston, Texas, wearing heavier clothes than needed. Temperature is over one hundred degrees, and humidity is near 100 percent. We check into the motel across the street from the famous Shamrock Hotel—a five minute walk from the Texas Medical Center and Baylor College of Medicine.

The first thing tomorrow, we must find a store to buy summer clothes and locate our rented home. In two days, we will collect our luggage and boxes we had to leave on the train. I am proud of my husband, Will's, many accomplishments, and I am proud of our children. They remained calm, gracious, and lovable throughout an unanticipated and frightening situation. I am grateful; I am on my knees thanking our Heavenly Father for blessing our family.

HOUSTON,
TEXAS

Houston is entirely a new experience! We have no car. We walk, ride the bus, or take a taxi. To collect our things left on the train and take them to our new rented house, we ride a taxi. The bus is another story. The first time on a Houston bus, my husband helped an elderly black lady into the bus and to a seat close to the front. The bus driver yelled very rudely at him, "Wada ya think you're doin'?" He then shouts at the person my husband had treated so kindly, "Get to the back seat, lady, or leave the bus." We found our way to Montgomery Ward store to buy some summer shorts and tees for the children. Before leaving the store, the manager yelled at the children, "Don't you know the rules? You do not drink at the colored's fountain." We have a lot to learn!

The rented house that was made ready for us by Baylor College of Medicine's Dr. Burdon is lovely. Our furniture has been delivered; since we have very few items for the living and dining rooms, we can appreciate the beautiful parquetry floors. We are busy getting bedrooms arranged; the children are discovering their personal treasures as we unpack. They are going from room to room to inspect their new home.

We have been told we should turn on the attic fan and open one or two windows—no more than that—and let the fan bring in fresh air. There is no air conditioning.

A neighbor comes to our door. Will goes to the door and learns we are in a Jewish neighborhood. Turns out that the neighbor owns a men's clothing store. He had seen us arrive and saw my husband wearing rather heavy clothes for Houston weather. He had also noted we had no car and offered to take him to his store on a day that Will would like to go. We invite him in, and Will introduces his family. We have a new friendly neighbor.

As he leaves, two ladies come and ring our doorbell. One has a basket on her arm, and the other has a bouquet of flowers. They are faculty wives welcoming us to Baylor, bringing a basket containing our dinner and flowers. When they see the bare rooms, Kathryn says, "I have a friend in Galveston who is selling her rattan furniture and some other items. They are like new. The rugs are from India—black with hand-embroidered colorful flowers. They would look beautiful on your parquetry floors. Would you like me to call her and find if she still has everything? If you'd like to see what she has, I'll be happy to drive you. I'll call you tomorrow."

Fortunately, our phone is connected, and arrangements have worked out well. Will and I have lovely rattan furniture with cushions and a table and also numdah rugs, which we got at a very good price, delivered. There are many things we need.

Tomorrow Will goes to his new office. He tells me, "Audsie, you and the children need to know I'm going to be very busy getting settled into the new position I've accepted. I am anxious to meet my colleagues here and get to know the people I'll be working with at different hospitals and medical associations and to make new commitments and friends. I'll be leaving early every day, but I'll always be home for dinner with you and the kids.

I'm looking forward to taking you and the children to Baylor to introduce my lovely family to everyone. I learned from Dr. Burdon there's a faculty wives organization. His wife is looking forward to introducing you there."

"Honey, I am so proud of you and want you to know you'll be in my prayers that all will be a joy for you and for all of us. It's like a new beginning. New friends and new schools for the children will be a big change for them also." We hug and laugh as we agree that "we'll still be riding buses for a while." Fortunately, I can walk the children to their schools.

Time is going so quickly cause there's so much going on all at once. I'm sitting on the floor unpacking our books. I see the need for some bookcases. I'm making the orange crates do the job until we can get some decent ones.

Top priority is for Will to have some new clothes. During the years on the GI Bill, the veterans at Badger Village wore army clothes: boots, gloves, caps, and jackets. Those clothes served well. Now is a different need and a different time.

Our neighborhood is the best. When we step out our backdoor and into the big yard, we see the huge tree with the treehouse built into its heart. There's a ladder leading up to it. Our neighbors across the yard are generous and often bring us eggs. They own a poultry business.

One day they present a huge egg to young Will. He is told, "You now have a duck egg, and if you and your mom or dad can help you set up a warm place and a light bulb—an incubator—you'll hatch a baby duck." Willie comes in, carefully carrying his duck egg ready for me to help him. I suggest we make a warm place then go and ask our neighbor if they might have a small incubator we may borrow.

They have exactly what we need. Our whole family is very excited over young Willie's new project. The neighbors across the street have a son named Ronnie. He comes to our yard often to play. They make movies with Daddy Will's movie camera and climb to the playhouse in the tree. We all have a great time watching the temperature gauge on the incubator.

Ronnie's parents often invite us over to play Mahjong or cards. All our neighbors own businesses or are professionals. The Orthodox Jewish family has two daughters who offer to babysit for us.

Our first Christmas in Texas is very different. We have gardens in full bloom instead of snow blizzards and snowplows. We open a charge account at Foley's, and for the first time, we are able to buy on credit some truly special gifts. Example: a Lionel electric train, white ice skates, a baby doll and carriage, a camel hair coat for Will, and some clothes for Karen and Mom. The tab? Over three hundred dollars! We had it paid in three months and established good credit at Foley's.

Will continues his polio research knowing the project is closer to finding the vaccine for polio. Will's knowledge of the immune system is known. He is consultant to MD Anderson, Methodist, and Memorial Hospitals. He is very concerned about the unbelievable conditions at Jeff Davis , a city of Houston Hospital for charity and colored patients.

The children and I have been asked to come along to Baylor College of Medicine to meet everyone. We have met Dr. Burdon, the head of Will's department. Mae Lewis, his secretary, is delightful and tells us, "Dr. Fahlberg's students tell me how much they love his classes. He's an excellent teacher with a great sense of humor."

One of Will's students is leaving. His application for a preceptorship at a hospital in Massachusetts has been approved. He asked, "Dr. Fahlberg, I have a Chevy I'd like to sell. I learned you had no car. Would you like to take it off my hands? I won't need it—won't have time to keep it up. I'll sell it to you for a hundred dollars." Needless to say, we have a car! It's a four-door, two-seater black Chevy in fine shape. It will serve us well. I'm taking driving lessons. It feels good to have a car. No more bus transfers are needed for Will to get around. This Chevy is a jewel; it works great and has been treated well.

We're getting invitations to parties and to join clubs, churches, and PTAs. The children are making friends. Things are looking good; we open a savings account. The Lord has blessed us with good health and lots of love. I have joined the faculty wives club; Will has joined the doctors club where the family is always welcome. Lately, Will has been telling me about a veteran's opportunity to buy a house and have a 4 percent loan. He is interested; I am encouraged! We are getting all the information, and we are praying that it will be possible. A duck has hatched; we named him Quank.

1952

1952

1952 is a new beginning in a very special way. The Lord has blessed us with a son born in October. We have named him after his two grandfathers, Lawrence David. We are now a family of six.

Our modest home purchased with a VA loan at 4 percent interest is near the Texas Medical Center, where Baylor College of Medicine is located. Schools, a park with a playground, a baseball diamond, and a large swimming pool are within walking distance.

A small playhouse has been placed in our backyard. The landscaping has been accomplished by family and friends. We have a car!

Willson Fahlberg Sr 1946
Will had just returned home after serving as a combat medic
with the Tenth Mountain Division in Italy during WWII

1947. Audrey Fahlberg, President of Badger Village Wives Club
John Smith, President of Badger Village Association
Lawrence Halle, Director of Housing for the University of Wisconsin
University Officials

The Wisconsin State Journal

Member of Lee Newspaper Group

Don Anderson........ Publisher	Harold E. McClelland, State Editor
Roy L. Matson.......... Editor	John Canny. . Circulation Manager
Lawrence H. Fitzpatrick, City Editor	A. M. Brayton.... Editor-Emeritus

Entered as second class matter at the postoffice at Madison, Wis., under the act of March 3, 1879.

Mail subscription rates in Wisconsin: $8 a year; $4.50 for six months; 90 cents a month, payable in advance. Other rates on request.

Home delivered rates in Madison, 25 cents a week, payable to the carrier weekly; $1.10 per month; $3.25 for three months in advance; $6.50 for six months in advance and $13 for a year in advance.

Sunday, Mar. 7, 1948

Badger Village

It May Look Drab, But Vets, Wives Dress Place Up with Friendliness

By MRS. WILSON FAHLBERG
(Badger Village)

University of Wisconsin—Badger Village, reads the sign at the side of Highway 12 and 13, 35 miles north of Madison.

The motorist may see it and say, "University housing — way out here"? And may add, "And did you notice? no trees"!

Yes, to the casual passerby Badger may look drab, but the ex-GI thinks as his bus turns into the village, **"Boy is it good to be home."**

* * *

Perhaps the first thoughts of all prospective residents agree with Burton Immen, the real estate dealer, who said of one of his houses — "There are possibilities here for someone with a little imagination and courage."

Ambition may be added as being mighty important. The first thing most wives feel like doing when they arrive, baby, bags, and baggage, is to sit down and cry.

The feeling of aloneness, isolation, and distance overwhelms one at first, but after getting settled it's that very feeling of aloneness that makes one desire friends.

Mrs. Willson Fahlberg
Karen and Willson Jr.
1948

Welcome to Rabbitville: After World War II, Badger Village helped house UW-Madison's own little baby boom as married students (above) flocked to universities on the GI Bill

Dr. Willson Fahlberg and wife Audrey
Retirement Party - Baylor College of Medicine 1989

DON ANDERSON : *publisher*
ROY MATSON : *editor*

A fact finding newspaper
the wisconsin state journal

March 9, 1948

madison
wisconsin

Mrs. Wilson Fahlberg
Badger Village,
Wisconsin

Dear Mrs. Fahlberg:

Many thanks for the fine guest editorial which appeared
in The Wisconsin State Journal last Sunday, March 7th.

I thought you might want to keep the enclosed glossy
print for your scrap book.

Sincere best wishes.

Yours very truly,

ROY L. MATSON, Editor.   /hsh

encl.

member lee newspaper group

OFFICE OF THE DIRECTOR

March 8, 1948

Mrs. Wilson Fahlberg
University Badger Project
Badger, Wisconsin

Dear Mrs. Fahlberg:

I enjoyed very much your guest editorial in the Wisconsin State
Journal on March 7. I think you did a fine job portraying life
at Badger, and I know that Badger Village has only been possible
because of individuals like you who were willing to work in making
it a community. I, too, am proud of Badger Village--certainly not
because of the buildings and facilities--but because of the people
who live in them and the excellent community spirit, ingenuity,
and enthusiasm.

Again, congratulations on your fine article and thanks for all
of your work at Badger.

Sincerely,

Lee Burns, Director

LB:ai

I acknowledge my daughter Karen's letter dated May 07, 2017, encouraging me to write this book and my whole family cheering me on at age ninety-seven.

And thanks to this team working together to make it a (third) published book:

Mary Flores—Publishing Consultant
Emman Villaran—Manuscript Services and Copyediting
Joy Daniels—Submissions Representative
Renee Ashton—my Editor who worked with me hours and days
Allen Lyon—author's photo